Aging Gracefully

Helpful Hints for the Elderly

— Isaiah 40:31 —

*But they who wait for the Lord shall renew
their strength;*

They shall mount up with wings like eagles;

They shall run and not be weary;

They shall walk and not faint.

Aging Gracefully

Helpful Hints for the Elderly

Diane E. Dunn

THREE SKILLET

AGING GRACEFULLY: HELPFUL HINTS FOR THE ELDERLY,
Dunn, Diane E.
1st ed.

––––––––––––

Books by Diane Dunn:
Aging Gracefully: Helpfully Hints for the Elderly
Organizing Your Home Office for a More Successful You
Life Untangled: Living Better by Living Easier
One Layover at a Time: Tips for Traveling Well
Making Summer Count: Hints for Your Best Summer Ever

Diane's books are available from Three Skillet Publishing, Amazon, and from Diane at her website, www.dianedunn.org.

––––––––––––

––––––––––––

♠♣♠ THREE SKILLET

www.ThreeSkilletPublishing.com

ISBN: 978-1-943189-90-8

A Note from Diane

Satisfaction in life is accepting what comes our way. As children, it's the new and different. *What's coming up? We want to be there. There, that, that's what I want to become!*

It doesn't have to be any different for us as we mature into our senior years. We may have enjoyed activities and people that we can never return to, but that doesn't mean we don't have an exciting future still out there in front of us.

Aging Gracefully is a guide into that future. In this latest book offering helpful hints for a better and improved life, I've included reminders and suggestions that can help you (or your loved one!) navigate this unfamiliar territory with grace and aplomb.

Here's what I'd like you to do: Take this book one section at a time and see which hints most apply to you. Don't try to incorporate all of them into your life all at once. That's impossible. Two or three, take those and see if they work for you. Then, when you've settled into those changes, revisit that section in this book and see if you are ready to try another of my hints.

You see, your life hasn't brought you to where you are all at once, and the hints I'm suggesting to help you age gracefully don't need to happen overnight. They are simply suggestions, ideas to get you thinking about your future so that you can be as happy, as independent, and as excited about the rest of your life as you were as a child.

This is your life. Make the most of it. Enjoy every moment. I truly hope the hints I've included in this book will help you to do exactly that.

Sincerely,
Diane Dunn
www.dianedunn.org

Table of Contents

Around the House

Age is an issue of mind over matter. If you don't mind, it doesn't matter!

— Psalm 71:9 —

"Do not cast me off in the time of old age; forsake me not when my strength is spent."

Around the House

Hint No. 1

Embrace Simplicity

Scale back your home, your purses, your closets, any clutter around you. Keep what makes you happiest and let the rest go. Even your obligations. If they don't make you happy, life is too short to do things you don't like. This is your life. Live it in the way that's best for you.

Around the House

Hint No. 2

Keep a List

Everyone who provides care for you, in or out of your home, should be on it. Include their phone numbers so they will be easy to contact in an emergency. You can also use this list to organize when each person shows up to keep from becoming overwhelmed.

Around the House

Hint No. 3

Toss Out Your Candles

Exposed flames are a breathing hazard, and if the house catches fire, you may not be able to move fast enough to escape. Then there's the smoke that can overwhelm you. It's not worth it.

Around the House

Hint No. 4

In Case of a Fire

Keep low if you must exit a burning structure. It's usually the smoke that kills (even grease on the stove). If clothing catches fire, stop, drop, and roll to put out the fire.

Around the House

Hint No. 5

Donate that Chair

Haven't used that chair in over a year?
Donate it or discard it. You'll appreciate
the extra room, and your visitors will, also.
Your donation can help your favorite
charity and free you from holding onto
what you don't use.

Around the House

Hints No. 6-7

Tape Your Floor Mats

If you must use bath floor mats, apply rug tape under the corners. Your bath will look pretty and be safe, also!

Only Take On What You Can

Cleaning tasks can become monumental as we age. If you see that your plans have outgrown your ability, call someone for help before you tackle a big job!

Around the House

Hint No. 8

Front Door Security

If your door doesn't have a peep hole, they are easy to install with a properly sized drill bit. Keep safe. Be aware. Don't risk opening your house to strangers. Know who's at your door!

Around the House

Hint No. 9

Safety at the Sink

Rubberized faucet covers can prevent burns. As we age, our response to pain can dim, and we can't move our hand away fast enough. They also make the faucet easier to turn on and off.

Around the House

Hint No. 10

Space Heater Safety

Give away your space heaters and turn up the furnace. If you must use one, use your yardstick to keep it three feet away from anything that might burn. Safety before "that's the way I've always done it." Don't burn your house down in a cold spell.

Around the House

Hint No. 11

Smoke Detector Batteries

Change your smoke and carbon monoxide batteries seasonally. Ask a neighbor, or your city help line can suggest a service that can do this for you. Share a plate of cookies when your volunteer shows up at your door.

Around the House

Hint No. 12

Seeing Where You Walk

Replace outdoor bulbs that light walkways or doors. They are vital for your safety at night. Ask a neighbor to help you test your lights regularly to see which ones need attention. Repeat as needed for nighttime safety!

Around the House

Hint No. 13

Colorful Keys

Color code your keys to locate the right one easily. You can buy custom keys or use fingernail polish to match them to your door or clothing! Repaint as necessary if your paint or polish wears thin.

Around the House

Hint No. 14

Check Your Throw Rugs

Throw rugs are pretty but easy to trip over. Only use them if they have a rubber backing. Better, remove them all for a safer at-home experience! Your elbows and knees will thank you.

Around the House

Hints No. 15-16

Cleaning Slippers Are a Must

Cleaning slippers can save your back and give you shining floors at the same time! If they seem silly, use them when no one else is around.

No Lock Unlocked

Check your windows once a week to ensure none are left unlocked. This is especially important in nice weather when windows are opened more.

Around the House

Hint No. 17

Hallway Navigation

Install nightlights in the hallways and bathrooms. Choose an LED version and they'll consume almost no electricity. You'll navigate your way easier than ever without bumping any walls! You'll "skip the light fantastic."

Around the House

Hint No. 18

Let Your Phone Answer for You

Take your time getting to the phone. There's no call important enough to risk a fall. That's what answering machines are for. You'll save yourself a knock on the knee or a toppled shelf, and that's good for everyone.

Around the House

Hint No. 19

Keep Stairs Clear

Keep stairs clear of books or shoes, and make sure handrails are firmly attached. Then hold on as you go up and down the stairs. Have someone else carry your things if you need to transport heavy items between floors.

Around the House

Hint No. 20

Bathroom Upgrade

You can replace your toilet seat with a raised seat with handlebars. It will be easier to sit and stand when you need to go, keeping you safe and well in the privacy of your home. This is a place no one wants to require extra help.

Around the House

Hint No. 21

Add More Plugs

Check for extension cords and remove them from walkways. Reposition your electrical items or call an electrician if you need more plugs. The cost for extra outlets is less than a hospital stay should you trip and fall.

Around the House

Hint No. 22

Shower Seating

If you have room, a bathing chair in your shower can prevent falls. Keep a moisture-proof pair of slippers and a long-handled brush nearby. Cleaning your feet will never be easier.

Around the House

Hints No. 23-24

Your Digital Assistant

Alexa to the rescue! A digital assistant can send you reminders, play your favorite songs and allow you to feel more self-sufficient.

No More Scalded Skin

Set your water heater to 120 degrees or less. Call your electric company to see how. They might even come and do it for you!

Around the House

Hint No. 25

Measure Your Walking Space

Use a yardstick to ensure you have at least 32 inches of access between items of furniture. That's the minimum for a walker or wheelchair. You will no longer need to worry about getting where you want to go!

Around the House

Hint No. 26

Sharpen Soft Corners

Soften sharp corners on furniture with stick-on pads to prevent tears in tender skin. You can also buy moldable putty that dries into rubber and can be safely removed later.

Around the House

Hint No. 27

Organize Those Small Items

Place clutter (newspapers, loose clothes, shoes) in plastic boxes or laundry baskets so they aren't tripping hazards. You'll appreciate the organization, and you'll walk safer when you do.

Around the House

Hint No. 28

Tub Cleaning Simplified

A broom works well for cleaning the shower or tub. Spray the end with bathroom cleaner and work it across every surface. You'll be able to reach even the tightest corners.

Around the House

Hint No. 29

Balance First

Install grab bars near your toilet and shower. You will feel more secure as you move about when you don't have to navigate the shower threshold with wet feet while holding to a towel rod. No bathroom falls permitted!

Around the House

Hint No. 30

Toss Those Cords

If you find a frayed appliance cord on a small appliance, toss the appliance out. Most small appliances are easily replaced. Your house after an electrical fire isn't.

The Kitchen

One benefit of old age is that your secrets are safe with your friends — they can't remember them either!!

— Leviticus 19:32 —

"You shall ... honor the face of an old man, and you shall fear your God: I am the Lord."

The Kitchen

Hint No. 1

Add These to Your Fridge

Check your phone number list on the fridge. Include 911 (even if it seems obvious), poison control, a family member or friend, and the healthcare provider's office. Use large letters and numbers. Under stress, even familiar numbers can be difficult to see or recall.

The Kitchen

Hints No. 2-3

Roll Up Those Sleeves

Remove loose clothing when cooking.
Even long sleeves can be a hazard
around your cookstove.

Get a Grip

An easy-grip jar opener can get you into
those too-tight jars. A rubber glove also
works well.

The Kitchen

Hint No. 4

Salt Alternatives

Spices, lemon, and fresh herbs can replace salt in foods for that extra zing of flavor. Look for low-sodium canned foods, especially deli meats and even carbonated beverages. They can all come loaded with salt.

The Kitchen

Hints No. 5-6

Cook for Two

Cook ahead and freeze food to reheat in the microwave. If you can no longer cook, have someone do this for you.

Bring the Back to the Front

A turntable in your cabinets can move those hidden items in the back into easy reach with a simple push of a finger.

The Kitchen

Hint No. 7

Keep Greens Available

Check your refrigerator weekly to ensure you have a selection of high-fiber fruits and vegetables for your daily meals. Don't forget to drink a full glass of liquid with every meal.

The Kitchen

Hints No. 8-9

Fortify Your Diet

Remember to select fat-free or low-fat milk for the vitamin D, or choose fortified non-dairy products if dairy doesn't agree with you.

Try Out Your Broiler

Learn to broil instead of fry. You can still get that crispy crunch, and your heart and cholesterol will thank you.

The Kitchen

Hints No. 10-11

Your Lazy Fridge

Have you installed a Lazy Susan in the fridge? The space you lose will be replaced by the items you can easily access. Do it now!

Easy Access Phone

You've posted your emergency numbers on the fridge. Place a phone nearby for easy access dialing.

Mealtime

Now that we've become seniors, everything's starting to click for us! Our knees, our backs, our necks . . .

— Job 12:12 —

"Wisdom is with the aged, and understanding in length of days."

Mealtime

Hint No. 1

Indulge Occasionally

Feel free to indulge in your favorite "guilty" foods, but only occasionally and in small amounts. Buy a single slice of pie, the small container of ice cream, or an individual candy bar. Leave the larger portions for those who can afford the extra calories and sugar.

Mealtime

Hints No. 2-3

Eat Regularly

Don't skip meals. Eat small but eat something. Your body may not adjust well to irregular mealtimes.

The Perfect Snack

Canned fruit (in metal cans or individual plastic containers) makes a great, healthy snack.

Mealtime

Hint No. 4

Hydration Is Key

If water's not your thing, snack on cucumbers, melons, and grapes. These are mostly water and will give your skin the hydration it needs for your most youthful look.

Mealtime

Hint No. 5

Make Two Meals from One

Don't think you need to eat the full meal when ordering at a restaurant. Most establishments offer to-go boxes, and you can enjoy the rest of your meal the next day.

Mealtime

Hints No. 6-7

All Food Groups

Plan an item from each food group for every meal. If you can't, a daily multiple vitamin will keep your nutrients rounded out.

Focus on the Green

For one meal a day, focus on fruits and vegetables. You'll up your vitamins, minerals, and antioxidants … and your weight might improve, too!

Mealtime

Hints No. 8-9

Straw Control

Use a clothespin and tape to keep your straw from moving around your glass. When the cup moves, the straw won't!

Focus on Your Food

Turn off the TV when eating. If you have someone to talk with, carry on a conversation. If not, open the blinds and see what's going on outside.

Health

The only thing that comes to you without effort is old age.

— Proverbs 16:31 —

"Gray hair is a crown of glory; it is gained in a righteous life."

Health

Hint No. 1

Sugar Warning Ahead!

Watch out for foods with lots of calories but few nutrients. If the label says "added sugars," or has solid fats such as butter, lard, or margarine, or is high in sodium (salt), it may not be the best choice for you.

Health

Hints No. 2-3

Bulk Up on "D"

A vitamin D supplement will ward off that dreaded osteoporosis diagnosis. Add calcium to your supplement, and you can reduce bone loss by almost half.

Shoulders High!

Good posture can take years from your looks. You may also prevent back pain by simply standing up straight.

Health

Hint No. 4

An Eye on the Small Things

Medication management is difficult for anyone, especially seniors who may take multiple medications. Changes in reaction speed, appetite, or drowsiness after medication changes needs to be reported to your physician immediately.

Health

Hints No. 5-6

Don't Put Off That Flu Shot

Don't forget your seasonal vaccinations against flu or pneumonia. Many providers will cover these at no charge to you.

Before You Feel Sick

Don't forget to schedule preventative healthcare visits. Even if you feel nothing is wrong, your doctor may discover something you hadn't noticed.

Health

Hints No. 7-8

Don't Skip the Physical

A full body physical is important for your doctor to screen for issues you may not notice. Your physician will know the signs and can alert you what to watch for.

Virtual Doctor Visits

Try FaceTime with your healthcare professional. A virtual appointment can be useful and easy once you know how.

Health

Hints No. 9-10

Turn Up the Light

Use a bright lamp to read your medication labels. Never open and consume medication in a darkened room.

Early to Bed ...

Keeping a regular bedtime schedule will help you to sleep better and more soundly at night. It will also encourage you to get a full night's sleep (at least 7-9 hours).

Health

Hint No. 11

No Smoking Allowed

Toss out the temptation to smoke. Cigarettes, cigars, and pipes can attack skin elasticity (wrinkles … organ function!) and contribute to cancer, strokes, and heart failure. That doesn't have to be you unless you let it.

Health

Hints No. 12-13

Don't Repackage Medications

Keep your medications in their original containers, except when sorting them into your weekly pill organizer. It doesn't do to mix and match medications!

Ask Your Pharmacist's Help

Bring all your pill bottles to your pharmacy. Your pharmacist can determine if you are taking them correctly.

Health

Hint No. 14

Fancy It Up

Tired of rows of pill bottles on your kitchen table or dresser? A new jewelry box is an attractive way to sort your medications. Purchase a pretty one, and you won't mind keeping your medications handy (even on the coffee table!).

Personal Care

Don't let aging get you down; it's too hard to get back up!

— Isaiah 40:29 —

"He gives power to the faint, and to him who has no might he increases strength."

Personal Care

Hint No. 1

Taking Care of the Outside

Visit a dermatologist rather than a spa. Sure, a spa treatment is okay occasionally, but a dermatologist can offer skin treatment options that can peel years (literally) from your looks. Give it a try today.

Personal Care

Hint No. 2

Get a Dentist's Opinion

Don't discount your dentist. Bright, white teeth can take years off your smile. Your dentist can assure you keep your teeth – or offer you options for replacement if one can't be saved!

Personal Care

Hint No. 3

Hand Spa Treatment

Tend to your hands. They receive the roughest abuse of any part of our bodies, from frequent washing to sun exposure. Your nails, too. Lotion, anti-aging creams, and cuticle softeners all work well. You can get low-gloss nail strengthener if you don't like that "polished" look.

Personal Care

Hints No. 4-5

Banish that Frown

Avoid frowning. It will add furrows between your brows. A smile will lift your face and help you appear younger.

Your Best Outdoor Friend

Sunscreen is your outdoor friend. Be sure to check the expiration date, because even the best sunscreens have a finite shelf life.

Personal Care

Hint No. 6

Anti-Aging Aisle – Bah!

Skip the anti-aging aisle in the drugstore. It seems counterintuitive, but a quality retinoid and daily moisturizers (in addition to your faithfully applied sunscreen) will be your best friends.

Personal Care

Hints No. 7-8

Support Your Feet

Wear sturdy shoes that give your feet plenty of support. If you have trouble tying laces, see if they come with easy-to-fasten Velcro straps.

Broad-Brimmed Hats Are Key

Cuts and bruises take longer to heal as we age. Protect yourself from the sun to avoid skin cancer or other skin complications.

Personal Care

Hints No. 9-10

Keep Track of Your Weight

Never avoid your scales. Your weight impacts your heath, from your joints to your breathing to your heart. Eating right and keeping active is key here.

Help on the Way!

Get a "fall alarm" that you can wear as a necklace or a bracelet. If you can't get to the phone, emergency services can still get to you!

Aging Gracefully
Helpful Hints for the Elderly

Personal Care

Hint No. 11

Saving the Soap

Old pantyhose cut in half prevents soap
from falling in the shower. Slip a bar of
soap inside and tie it to the shower head
or a grab bar. Your soap will suds up fine,
then it can air dry. You'll never have to
pick it up from the shower floor again.
Clean and safe, all in one.

Personal Care

Hint No. 12

Protect Your Emotional Health

Watch out for signs of elder depression, especially after a life-changing event, such as losing a loved one. Never ignore the warning signs.

If you are feeling down or struggling with making it through the day, speak with your doctor and explain that you don't know why you feel "in the dumps."

Age Proofed

Growing old is inevitable but growing up is optional!

— Philippians 1:6 —

"And I am sure of this, that he who began a good work in you will bring it to completion at the day of Jesus Christ."

Age Proofed

Hint No. 1

Be Physically Active

Any level of physical activity will help prevent illness and give you better sleep at night. If you must sit to rest, get moving again as soon as you can. Carry a portable stool with you, and you'll be surprised at where you can go and the things you will be able to do.

Age Proofed

Hints No. 2-3

Staying on Balance

Balance training as you age is as
important as muscle training. Get advice
on how to stand, place your feet, and stay
steady.

Walk with a Walker If Needed

Use a walker rather than holding onto
walls or furniture. You'll have better grip,
and your walker won't fall over on you
(unlike that TV or china cabinet).

Age Proofed

Hints No. 4-5

Use a Button Hook

A button hook tool will cinch up those pesky buttons easy-as-you-please. You can also use a button hook to pull zippers closed.

Rubber Bands Do the Trick

Wrap wide rubber bands around your cups and glasses to make them easier to grip. No more dropped glasses for you!

Age Proofed

Hints No. 6-7

Raised Stickers Are a Nice Touch

Add raised stickers to your remote controls or smart phone to help you feel which buttons you need to push, such as 9-1-1 or the on-and-off buttons.

The Joy of Large Print

A large-print keyboard will help you work your computer, even if your eyesight betrays you. The larger letters will be easier to see.

Age Proofed

Hint No. 8

Speak in French

How about a foreign language? Learn a phrase in French or Spanish. Use it when you are out and about. You'll enjoy showing off your new skill, and you'll be seen as a "smart" world traveler (even if you aren't).

Age Proofed

Hint No. 9

Use the Camera on Your Phone

Use your smartphone to take a picture of where you park, the gas pump display when the receipt doesn't print, or a street sign when you need to ask for directions. There's no cost to take as many as you want, and you'll never forget anything again!

Age Proofed

Hints No. 10-11

Use Your Phone as a Magnifier

Use your smartphone as a magnifier. Go to Settings, then Accessibility, and tap the Magnifier to adjust your settings.

Get an Outside Viewpoint

Arrange home visits by your healthcare provider. Seeing you in your home can help them offer suggestions to keep you in your home.

Age Proofed

Hints No. 12-13

Ease Up on the Salt

When you purchase nuts, check the package for the unsalted variety. They will taste sweeter and do their part to keep your blood pressure under control.

Make the Best Food Choices Possible

Healthy eating is your obvious choice to prevent declining health or disabilities. Exercise and reduced stress also play a part.

Mental Wellness

The older the fiddle, the sweeter the tune!

— Ruth 4:15 —

"He shall be to you a restorer of life and a nourisher of your old age."

Mental Wellness

Hint No. 1

On the Cutting Edge

Be a trendsetter. Read a fashion magazine. Learn what's on the cutting edge. You don't have to adopt all of it. No one does. Just pick a small part and get out in front of the crowd. It can be your "secret sauce" bolstering your confidence for the day.

Mental Wellness

Hints No. 2-3

You Are More than Your Age

Live in the moment, not by remembering how you looked in the mirror when you woke up. You think you are your reflection, but others see how much they enjoy your personality and your vibrance.

Give the Present Your Attention

Be engaged, not distracted. Be present, not wistful. Be connected, not preoccupied with yesterday or tomorrow.

Mental Wellness

Hints No. 4-5

Your Response Is Key

What will happen will happen. How you respond is up to you. Take charge of now and you will take charge of your future in the process.

Get Out There!

Take a trip to somewhere new. Call your local senior center to see if they have any adventures planned.

Mental Wellness

Hint No. 6

Put Yourself in Control

Let your gray hair become your calling card. Embrace it. Your confidence is what people will notice. You might mourn your lost youth, but others will see your strength in your boldness. Take charge of your life, no matter your age. Your years don't own you. You own your years, so be proud of them.

Mental Wellness

Hint No. 7

Style Yourself Up

You can't change the way you age, but you can style up the way you dress. Add something bright and fresh to your wardrobe each time you step out the door. A scarf, a fresh shirt in a bright color, or a pink belt. People will notice your clothes, not the lines in your face, and you will feel more confident in yourself.

Mental Wellness

Hint No. 8

Think Young to Be Young

Be optimistic. Act as though you are, even if you don't feel it. As people compliment you on your attitude, you will find yourself feeling the upbeat surge of confidence that comes with your new and changing outlook on life.

Mental Wellness

Hint No. 9

That Snooze Is Good for You

Sleep brings down stress. If you have a bad day, shut things down and take a nap. A full night's rest will be even better. It's good for you, and you will feel better afterward.

Mental Wellness

Hint No. 10

Fry Instead of Scramble

Vary the way you do things to keep your mind in tip-top shape. Fry your eggs instead of scramble. Work a new type of crossword. Take up miniature golfing instead of bowling. Do what interests you.

Mental Wellness

Hint No. 11

Keep Score of Your Successes

You can learn new skills at any age. Work a crossword. Do a wordsearch. Assemble a puzzle. Get out that set of dominoes and KEEP SCORE. You will find yourself remembering more and more as you go.

Aging Gracefully
Helpful Hints for the Elderly

Mental Wellness

Hints No. 12-13

Nature Is Good for You

Spend time in nature, even if it is just a walk in your yard. Being outdoors can refresh your thoughts and offer you a new outlook on the day.

Take On a New Hobby

Take on a new hobby or restart one you used to love. You can register at your local junior college to take a class, perhaps even for free!

94

Mental Wellness

Hint No. 14

Dominoes, Anyone?

Play a "brain game" a day to invigorate your mind. Work a crossword. Read. Tell a story. Even dominoes help the brain stay sharp by keeping track of the numbers as you play!

Being with other people you enjoy? A priceless benefit that will do you wonders.

Mental Wellness

Hints No. 15-16

Pay Attention to Yourself

If you have a medical emergency, you may battle with depression afterward. Be familiar with the warning signs and ask for help.

Have Realistic Expectations

Focus on what you can do, not what you can't; and the people you still have around, not those you don't. Life is still full of opportunity no matter your age.

Mental Wellness

Hint No. 17

Taking Life in Stride

Make a funny drawing about things that frustrate you. (Simple is better! It's just for you.) Put it on the refrigerator. After a week, you can tear it in half and toss it away. Make another if you are still frustrated. You will improve your mood each time.

Family and
Relationships

*Instead of "hot flashes," think of it as
your inner child playing with matches.*

— Proverbs 17:6 —

"Grandchildren are the crown of the aged,
and the glory of children is their fathers."

Family and Relationships

Hint No. 1

Enjoy a Grandkids Night

Invite your grandchildren to spend the night. The shared activities of making dinner or watching a favorite movie will lift your spirits. If overnight is too much, take them out for a burger or ice cream. That little bit of time will be a memory you will treasure.

Family and Relationships

Hint No. 2

Choose a Chore

If you live with family, claim a chore you are certain you can do. Fold clothes. Run the vacuum. Whatever you feel you can do on an ongoing basis. You will feel useful, and your family will value your presence in the house.

Family and Relationships

Hint No. 3

Join Family Outings

Always say yes when family members invite you on an outing. Weddings, birthdays, try to be there for each one. If you don't receive a call, ask to be included!

Family and Relationships

Hint No. 4

Even If You Can't Ride Along ...

Join in group activities even if you can't get out of the house. Zoom, Facebook, even your smart phone's camera will get you where you want to go when you must remain at home. Stay involved, and you will enjoy each day a little more.

Family and Relationships

Hint No. 5

The Post Office Comes to You!

Send cards or make calls to your healthcare providers to celebrate holidays or birthdays. They will think of you often (and perhaps give you more attentive care!).

Family and Relationships

Hint No. 6

Friends Are Your Best Bonus

Determine an activity you can do with a group. It might be a walk, a boardgame, or heading out to a local eatery. You might be helping encourage someone else with your time and attention.

Family and Relationships

Hint No. 7

The Story of Your Life

Begin writing the story of your life. Concentrate on one month or year. Call a loved one and read what you've written. If they remember it differently, you've sparked a moment for spirited discussion. Yea for you!!

Family and Relationships

Hint No. 8

Don't Frustrate! Delegate!

If you've taken on a task, and you know you can't complete it, delegate! Don't be afraid to ask for help. Never say, "I can't." Instead, say, "I need you to do this part for me so that I can finish."

Family and Relationships

Hint No. 9

Give Others the Benefit of the Doubt

It's difficult to give up control as you age. Be prepared to show patience with your caregivers as they adjust to your new needs and expectations.

Finances and Living Alone

Wherever life takes you, go with all your heart!

— Psalm 90:12 —

"So teach us to number our days that we may get a heart of wisdom."

Finances and Living Alone

Hint No. 1

Know Where Your Insurance Stands

Keep current on your insurance options. Long-term care, life insurance, and increased or decreased levels of insurance might be affected by your current health level.

Finances and Living Alone

Hint No. 2

Have Regular Check-ups

Twice a year is a good schedule for vision exams, hearing tests, and other health screenings. Check with your insurance company to see what they will cover. Perhaps all of it as a wellness program incentive!

Finances and Living Alone

Hint No. 3

Share Your Phone Solicitations

Talk over phone offers or Internet offers with family members before saying yes. They can offer you fresh insight and space to rethink the offer before you agree to something you wish you hadn't. Never share information with anyone you don't personally know or trust.

Finances and Living Alone

Hint No. 4

Share Your Life with a Pet

A pet, even a fish, can provide companionship and joy, increasing your overall health. They help you stick to a schedule (daily feedings!) and give you a long-range focus outside of yourself.

Finances and Living Alone

Hint No. 5

Volunteer to Help Others

If you miss your career, see if you can volunteer in a similar field. You'll still get joy out of doing a good deed, even if you no longer receive a paycheck, and others will benefit from what you spent a lifetime learning.

Finances and Living Alone

Hint No. 6

Make "Grateful Cards" to Share

Keep a stack of "grateful" cards out that tell things you enjoy about your life. Each day put a fresh one on top. Call someone, text them, even go on social media to mention your "grateful" card for the day. Then, tomorrow, do it all over again with the next card!

Finances and Living Alone

Hint No. 7

Work Your Strengths, Not Your Weaknesses

If mobility issues have you housebound, use your phone to keep up with life. Write a letter or two. Send greeting cards to people you may have lost contact with. You will enjoy the friendships you rebuild.

Finances and Living Alone

Hint No. 8

Make Yourself Indispensable

You need to feel useful. Fold clothes. Clip coupons. Make a grocery list. Prep foods for meals. Do what you can, even if it is keeping someone company while they run errands.

Finances and Living Alone

Hint No. 9

Don't Hold In Your Frustration

Express your feelings about aging, either with a close friend or by writing in a journal. "Getting it out" can prevent anger, resentment, or depression from building up.

Physical Activity

A retired husband is a wife's full-time job!

— Isaiah 46:4 —

"Even to your old age I am he, and to gray hairs I will carry you."

Physical Activity

Hint No. 1

Share Your Skills

Don't get caught up in what your age keeps you from doing. Look for things you can do and share those skills with others. Meaningful goals can make the difference between woe and go.

Physical Activity

Hint No. 2

The Little Things Count

Offer to water your neighbor's plants when they are out of town. Bake cookies for your Sunday school class. Run an errand for a homebound friend. You will feel better, and they will appreciate your help.

Physical Activity

Hint No. 3

Do Something Exciting

Take up a daring new hobby. Backpacking, cooking school, or swimming. Don't let aging strip you of your adventurous side. You can be as adventuresome as you want to be.

Physical Activity

Hint No. 4

Skip the Elevator

Taking the stairs instead of the elevator will increase blood flow to your skin, nourishing it for a better, healthier (and younger) look. Go slow (and check with your healthcare provider) if it is your first time. You will get better (and stronger) with practice.

Physical Activity

Hint No. 5

Get an Exercise Companion

Your motivation for exercise will decide if you continue. Get a pet that needs walked or schedule your weekly visit to the park with a friend. You will discover rekindled motivation when someone else depends on you to be there.

Physical Activity

Hint No. 6

Discover Your Options

Visit the gym or take a walk in the park two or more days a week. If you can't get out, ask your healthcare provider what you can substitute without leaving home. They will be able to share options with you.

Physical Activity

Hint No. 7

Start Small

For new physical activities, start slowly and work up to your desired goal. Mow one part of the yard. Walk halfway to the corner. Carry one bag in from the car. Soon, you'll be able to do more.

Physical Activity

Hint No. 8

Change the Game Play

If you can no longer exercise outside your home, see if you can bring your exercise home to you. There is exercise equipment specifically designed for seniors. Ask your healthcare provider for more information.

Physical Activity

Hint No. 9

Have a Backup Plan

When you discover you can no longer do a once-familiar activity, come up with an alternative. Kitchen knives a problem? Buy pre-sliced vegetables. Has the tub become difficult? Replace it with a walk-in shower. See? Your life might change, but it can still be lived to its fullest.

Physical Activity

Hints No. 10-11

Wear Nonslip Footwear

Wear nonslip footwear around the house. Slippers work well, or flat, thin-soled shoes can work. If you can feel the floor, you can maneuver with better ease!

Dance to the Music

Walk if you can. Clap to music, if that's all you can do. Just MOVE! You will sleep better and keep depression banished to the far side of the door.

Physical Activity

Hint No. 12

Here Are Five More Exercise Options:

1. Take a walk (just to the mailbox, if that's all you can do).

2. Sweep, mop, dust, or rake leaves.

3. Work in the garden or push the lawnmower.

4. Elongate thick rubber bands and gently release them.

5. Stretch with a friend. Encourage each other to touch those toes (or knees, if you can't).

Don't forget to share a pitcher of water when you exercise outside in a group and bring along a healthy snack for those energy lows. If you tire easily, you can practice chair yoga while you rest.

Focus Forward

How are stars like dentures? Both come out at night!

— Psalm 91:16 —

"With long life I will satisfy him and show him my salvation."

Focus Forward

Hint No. 1

Find Your Happy Spot

Learn what brings you happiness and peace. Make a list of when you were happiest. Pursue that. You won't get it all the time, but the anticipation will make the rest bearable.

Focus Forward

Hint No. 2

Dress for Your Best Look

Look for fabrics that fit your age. Clingy synthetics may be great for young people, but denim or wool may better suit your body at your age. Add a scarf or hat to finish the look. You will be the best you can be.

Aging Gracefully
Helpful Hints for the Elderly

Focus Forward

Hint No. 3

Do Something Important Every Day

You needn't "fall off a cliff" into retirement. Plan one item a day to achieve. Write a letter. Take the car to be washed. Walk the dog. Pick up your grandchild after school. Do something that requires your focus and attention. You will feel more fulfilled and useful when you do.

Focus Forward

Hint No. 4

Make a Change Others Notice

Change your hair color. Change your wallpaper. Buy a new car. Wear a style of clothes you've never considered before. Revise your style with an unusual pair of sunglasses. Embrace the new, older you by becoming a new you in a freshly creative way!

Focus Forward

Hint No. 5

Do Something You've Put Off

How about that cello you've always wanted to learn? Break out that old camera. Take a course in lawn mower repair. You have the ability. You just need to learn the skills. Be more than people tell you that you can be by learning something new!

Focus Forward

Hint No. 6

Wear Yourself Proudly

Don't rely on makeup. A little concealer for eye circles will do the trick. Keep the rest light. Over-applying will only accentuate fine lines. Accept your skin as a badge of your accomplishments. Love who you are.

Focus Forward

Hint No. 7

Never Misplace Your Keys Again

A "key finder" key ring will keep your keys in your possession. You can use your smart phone or tablet to track them down when they are "lost."

Focus Forward

Hint No. 8

Find Freedom in Who You Are

Don't get bogged down on getting older. You can't prevent it, so find the positive and focus on that. It might be the freedom of retirement or that you now have grandchildren you can spoil. Keep your thoughts on that.

Focus Forward

Hint No. 9

Make Your Wishes Clear

What extra care do you want, and when would you like to receive it? Let your caregiver know. They will be able to tailor their care to your needs. They want to be able to offer you the best care possible.

147

Focus Forward

Hint No. 10

Your Community Needs You!

Volunteer at your local senior community center. Or call your city hall and see where you can be useful. The skills you've learned over your lifetime are still there. Put them to use!

Focus Forward

Hint No. 11

Navigate Life's Minefields with Courage

A positive attitude is the best "lifter-upper" in old age. Emotional landmines will come with every new stage of life, but if you are prepared to navigate them, you can be happy into your golden years.

Turn the page to find more books by Diane Dunn

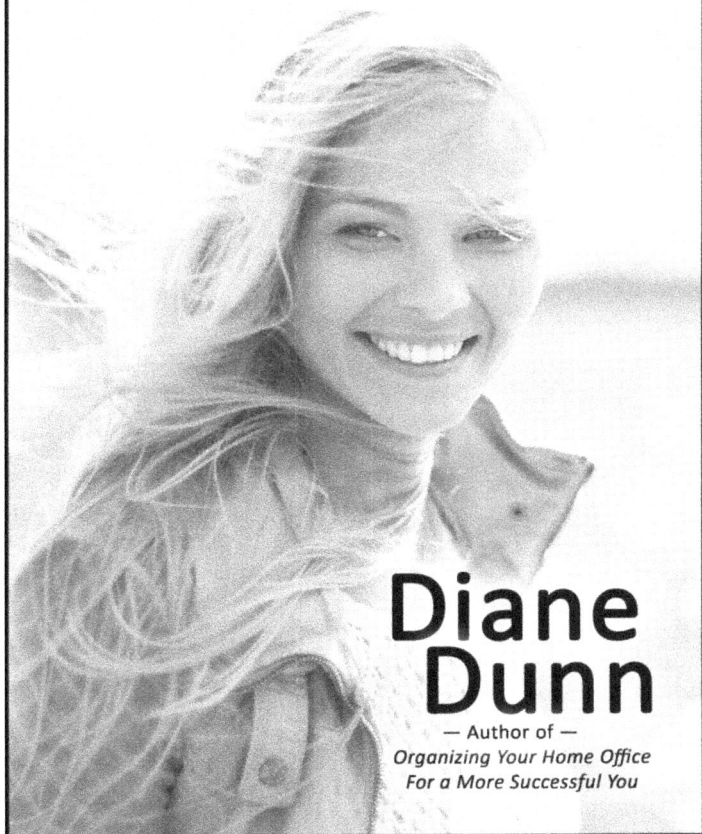

— You will look forward to your next journey! —

One Layover
at a
Time
— • —
Tips for Traveling Well

Diane
Dunn

Visit www.DianeDunn.org to order your copy today!

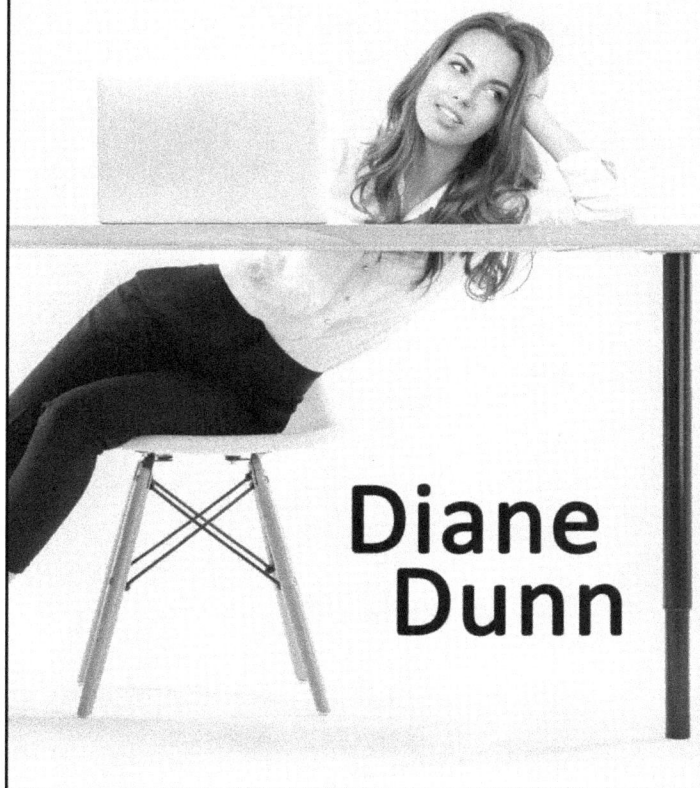

Making Summer Count

Hints for Your Best Summer Ever

Diane Dunn

Visit www.DianeDunn.org to order your copy today!

www.ingramcontent.com/pod-product-compliance
Lightning Source LLC
Chambersburg PA
CBHW060927040426
42445CB00011B/821